How to sell on eBay for beginners 2024

Your Definitive Guide to Profitable Selling

Scarlett Anderson

TABLE OF CONTENTS

INTRODUCTION

Welcome to the gateway of boundless opportunities: the world of eBay selling! In this immersive guide, we delve into the intricacies of mastering one of the largest online marketplaces, unveiling the art and science behind successful eBay entrepreneurship.

"How to sell on ebay for beginners 2024: Your Definitive Guide to Profitable Selling" is your compass in navigating the dynamic landscape of eBay, catering to beginners seeking a profitable entry and seasoned sellers aiming to amplify their online presence and sales.

The sheer enormity of eBay's global platform presents an unrivaled prospect for aspiring entrepreneurs. Whether you're a small business owner, an individual seller, or an established retailer looking to expand your digital footprint, this book equips you with the knowledge and strategies to thrive.

We embark on a journey starting with the essentials—establishing your seller account, crafting compelling listings, and understanding the nuances of eBay's interface. From there, we delve into the intricacies of successful sales strategies, exploring the dichotomy between auctions and fixed-price listings, unraveling the power of keywords and SEO, and harnessing the tools for optimal marketing and visibility.

But it's not merely about making sales; it's about building a sterling reputation. Providing exceptional customer service, cultivating trust, and managing feedback become your guiding principles as you navigate the realm of buyer-seller relationships.

As we progress, we unveil the complexities of managing your eBay business, diving into analytics, scaling strategies, and staying compliant with eBay's ever-evolving policies. Advanced techniques open doors to cross-promotions, international markets, and leveraging the platform's sophisticated features to elevate your selling game.

Yet, beyond the technicalities lies a roadmap for long-term success and sustainability. We offer insights into crafting resilient, adaptable strategies that withstand market fluctuations and propel your eBay venture toward enduring success.

In these pages, you'll find not just a manual but a blueprint—a comprehensive toolkit honed from the experiences and expertise of seasoned eBay sellers, designed to transform your aspirations into tangible, profitable outcomes.

So, fasten your seatbelt and embark on this exhilarating journey toward eBay excellence. This book is your guide, your mentor, and your steadfast companion as you unlock the doors to unparalleled success in the world of eBay selling.

CHAPTER ONE

Getting Started on eBay

eBay stands as an iconic pillar in the world of e-commerce, a digital marketplace that revolutionized how people buy and sell goods globally. Founded in 1995, eBay emerged as an innovative platform, transforming the traditional concept of auctions into a virtual hub for buying and selling an astonishing array of products.

At its core, eBay connects millions of buyers and sellers worldwide, offering a diverse spectrum of items spanning from electronics, fashion, collectibles, and beyond. Its unique blend of auction-style listings and fixed-price sales provides a dynamic environment where sellers can showcase their offerings in various formats, allowing buyers to bid or purchase immediately.

The platform thrives on a user-friendly interface, enabling individuals, small businesses, and large retailers alike to set up their virtual storefronts effortlessly. Sellers can craft detailed listings, complete with product descriptions, images, and pricing options, while buyers enjoy the convenience of exploring a vast array of products and making purchases from the comfort of their homes.

eBay's success hinges on its robust feedback and rating system, fostering trust between buyers and sellers. This system allows users to leave feedback based on their transaction experiences, contributing to a transparent and accountable marketplace.

Over the years, eBay has evolved, introducing sophisticated tools and features, including promotional tools, seller analytics, and global shipping options, empowering sellers to expand their reach and optimize their sales strategies.

With a global presence spanning numerous countries, eBay continues to be a vibrant, ever-evolving marketplace, offering opportunities for entrepreneurs to establish thriving businesses, collectors to find rare treasures, and shoppers to access an extensive array of products, all at their fingertips.

Creating Your eBay Seller Account

Creating an eBay account is a simple and quick process. It involves providing basic personal information, choosing a unique User ID, and agreeing to eBay's terms. Upon completion, users gain access to eBay's expansive marketplace for buying, selling, and engaging in various transactions. Here is a step by step guide on how to create your eBay seller account:

Step 1: Navigate to eBay's Website
Open your web browser and go to eBay's official website: www.ebay.com.

Step 2: Click on "Register"
On the eBay homepage, locate and click on the "Register" or "Sign Up" button. It's typically found at the top-left corner of the page.

Step 3: Enter Your Personal Information
You'll be directed to a registration page. Here, you'll need to enter your personal details, including your:
- First and last name
- Email address (preferably one you actively use)
- Create a secure password
- Phone number

Step 4: Verify Your Email

After entering your details, eBay will send a verification email to the email address you provided. Check your inbox (and your spam/junk folder) for an email from eBay and click on the verification link within the email.

Step 5: Enter Your Contact Information

Once your email is verified, return to eBay's website and log in using your email and password. eBay will then prompt you to enter your contact information, including your:

- Street address
- City
- State
- ZIP code
- Country

Step 6: Create a User ID

Next, you'll need to create a unique User ID that will be your identity on eBay. This ID will be visible to other users when you buy or sell items. Choose a name that reflects you or your business and isn't already in use by another eBay member.

Step 7: Review and Accept eBay's User Agreement

Carefully read through eBay's User Agreement and Privacy Policy. Once you've reviewed them, check the box to agree to the terms and conditions.

Step 8: Verify Your Phone Number (Optional)

eBay may request verification of your phone number for added security. Enter your phone number and follow the verification steps provided, such as receiving a code via text or call.

Step 9: Set Up Payment Method (Optional)

You can add a payment method, such as PayPal or a credit/debit card, for buying items on eBay. This step is optional during the initial account setup and can be completed later.

Step 10: Congratulations! You're Ready to Use eBay

Once you've completed these steps, you'll have successfully created an eBay account. You can now explore the platform, start buying items, or if you intend to sell, set up your seller account and begin listing your products.

Understanding eBay's Interface

eBay's interface is a dynamic and user-centric platform that seamlessly merges functionality with accessibility. With an intuitive layout and clear navigation, it presents a myriad of features—from detailed product listings to personalized account management—empowering users to effortlessly browse, buy, and sell. Its robust search tools and customizable dashboard offer tailored experiences, while communication channels and secure payment systems ensure smooth transactions. eBay's interface strikes a balance between simplicity and depth, fostering a user-friendly environment that caters to both novice and seasoned users, making the vast marketplace accessible to all.

This comprehensive page aims to equip readers with an in-depth understanding of eBay's multifaceted interface, enabling efficient navigation, optimal utilization of features, and an enriched experience while engaging with the platform's services.

1. Homepage Navigation:

Layout Overview: The Homepage showcases various sections, including featured listings, promotional banners, and categorized sections for easy browsing.
Search Functionality: The search bar offers advanced options and filters, allowing users to refine searches by price, condition, location, and more.

2. Account Dashboard:

Personalization Options: Users can manage preferences, notifications, and customize the dashboard for a tailored experience.
Activity Tracking: Access to the watchlist, purchase history, and saved searches for convenient monitoring and revisiting items of interest.

3. Listings Exploration:

Listing Page Features: Detailed listings display comprehensive product descriptions, multiple images, seller information, and bidding or purchasing options.
Search Optimization: Utilizing filters, sorting options, and saved searches to streamline product discovery and enhance user experience.

4. Buying and Bidding:

Auction Dynamics: Understanding bidding mechanisms, proxy bidding, and real-time auction updates for engaging bidding experiences.
Buy Now Options: Accessing fixed-price listings, best offers, and immediate purchase functionalities for efficient buying.

5. Selling on eBay:

Seller Dashboard Tools: Managing listings, orders, and accessing seller tools and resources for effective selling strategies.
Listing Creation: Step-by-step guidance for creating listings, leveraging selling features, and optimizing sales.

6. Communication Tools:

Messaging Features: Communication channels for buyers and sellers, managing inquiries, and negotiating terms within the platform.
Issue Resolution: Accessing the Resolution Center for dispute resolution and conflict management.

7. eBay's Payment System:

Payment Integration: Utilizing PayPal and other payment methods, managing invoices, and ensuring secure transactions.

Transaction Security: Safeguarding financial information and ensuring secure payments throughout the process.

8. My eBay Section:

Customization Options: Tailoring preferences, saved searches, and watchlist for a personalized and efficient browsing experience.

Order Management: Tracking orders, accessing order details, and managing returns within the My eBay section.

9. Mobile App Interface:

App Features Overview: Exploring eBay's mobile app functionalities and ensuring a seamless user experience across devices.

Consistency in Interface: Ensuring uniformity and functionality on various devices for ease of use.

10. Seller Tools and Analytics:

Seller Performance Hub: Analyzing sales metrics, utilizing reports, and tracking performance data for informed decision-making.

Promotions and Campaigns: Running promotional strategies using Promotions Manager and discounts.

11. Community and Help Resources:

Engagement Platforms: Accessing eBay's community forums for discussions, tips, and support from fellow users.

Help and Support Channels: Utilizing FAQs, customer service, and troubleshooting resources for assistance.

12. Security and Account Settings:

Account Protection: Implementing security measures, managing privacy settings, and ensuring the safety of personal information.
Profile Customization: Adapting account settings and preferences to suit individual needs.

13. Global Selling and International Interfaces:

Cross-Border Trade: Understanding international sites, language options, and currency considerations for global transactions.
Interface Adaptation: Navigating interfaces tailored for different countries and adapting to diverse global marketplaces.

14. Updates and Changes:

Interface Modifications: Staying informed about updates, new features, and changes introduced by eBay to adapt seamlessly.
Guidelines for Adaptation: Providing guidance and support for users to navigate and adapt to interface modifications.

CHAPTER TWO

Listing Your Products

As a seller, the art of presenting your products in the vast digital marketplace is a strategic journey that intertwines visibility, description, and strategic pricing. In this chapter, we embark on a comprehensive exploration of the intricate process of listing your products on eBay, transforming your inventory into captivating listings that entice buyers.

From selecting the right products to understanding market demand, optimizing titles, crafting compelling descriptions, and strategically setting prices, each step holds the key to attracting eager buyers. Capturing high-quality images, defining shipping options, and outlining clear return policies are the brushstrokes that paint a complete picture of trust and transparency for potential customers.

Beyond the creation of listings lies the art of visibility enhancement—utilizing eBay's promotional tools, leveraging SEO techniques, and exploring discounts to ensure your products stand out amidst the crowd. Effective communication strategies and meticulous monitoring of performance metrics become the compass guiding your listing journey toward success.

Get into the pages of this immersive expedition, where each detail matters, each strategy shapes your seller identity, and each listing becomes a beacon drawing buyers to your offerings. Together, we'll unravel the intricacies of eBay's platform, transforming your products into compelling listings that captivate, engage, and drive your sales to soaring heights.

Get ready to master the art of listing on eBay—an art that intertwines strategy, creativity, and precision to unlock the doors to unparalleled success in the world of e-commerce.

Optimizing Product Titles and Descriptions

Optimizing product titles and descriptions on eBay is pivotal for attracting potential buyers and ensuring your listings stand out in the vast marketplace. Here is a guide on how to effectively optimize product titles and descriptions for a unique listing in eBay's marketplace

Crafting Irresistible Product Titles:
- Clarity and Relevance: Create concise titles that accurately represent the item, including brand, model, size, color, and key features.
- Keyword Optimization: Incorporate relevant keywords that potential buyers are likely to search for, improving search visibility.
- Avoiding Misleading Information: Ensure titles accurately describe the item, avoiding exaggerated or misleading terms.

Crafting Compelling Product Descriptions:
- Detailed and Informative: Provide comprehensive yet succinct descriptions detailing product specifications, dimensions, condition, and any unique attributes.
- Use of Bullet Points: Organize information using bullet points for easy readability, highlighting key features and benefits.
- Addressing Buyer Concerns: Anticipate and answer potential buyer questions within the description to enhance confidence and reduce inquiries.

Key Elements of Effective Descriptions:
- Visual Descriptions: Complement text with high-quality images showcasing different angles, close-ups, and details of the product.
- Technical Specifications: Include precise measurements, materials used, technical specifications, and compatibility details when applicable.
- Unique Selling Proposition (USP): Highlight what sets your product apart from others, whether it's quality, exclusivity, or additional benefits.

SEO Strategies for eBay Listings:

Keyword Research: Utilize eBay's search bar to research relevant keywords and phrases commonly used by buyers searching for similar items.

Strategic Placement of Keywords: Incorporate selected keywords naturally within the title and description without overstuffing.

Enhancing Readability and Appeal:

Formatting: Use bold or italic fonts for emphasis, break text into paragraphs, and ensure a clean layout for easy reading.

Engaging Language: Use descriptive language that appeals to emotions while maintaining professionalism and accuracy.

Mobile Optimization:

Mobile-Friendly Descriptions: Craft descriptions that remain clear and legible on mobile devices, ensuring a seamless user experience across platforms.

A/B Testing and Refinement:

Continuous Improvement: Test different title and description formats, analyze their performance using eBay's analytics, and refine based on results.

Compliance and Honesty:

Accurate Representation: Ensure your titles and descriptions truthfully represent the product to avoid buyer dissatisfaction or disputes.

Adherence to eBay Policies: Comply with eBay's guidelines, avoiding prohibited content or practices in titles and descriptions.

By implementing these strategies, sellers can optimize their product titles and descriptions on eBay, maximizing visibility, attracting potential buyers, and ultimately increasing the likelihood of successful transactions in the dynamic online marketplace.

Setting Competitive Prices

Selling on eBay demands a delicate balance between profitability and market competitiveness. Here's a comprehensive strategy to master pricing:

1. Market Research and Analysis:
   - Competitor Assessment: Analyze similar listings to understand prevailing prices and market trends.
   - Price Range Identification: Determine a competitive range considering item condition, uniqueness, and demand.

2. Pricing Strategies:
   - Value-Based Approach: Align prices with the perceived value of your product, considering quality, brand, and features.
   - Profitability Consideration: Factor in costs, overheads, and desired profit margins when setting prices.

3. Leveraging eBay Tools:
   - Completed Listings Analysis: Use completed listings to evaluate actual selling prices and set realistic pricing benchmarks.
   - Best Offer Option: Enable negotiation flexibility while maintaining competitiveness.

4. Competitive Positioning:
   - Value Addition: Offer extra value through bundle deals, free shipping, or warranties to stand out.
   - Strategic Undercutting: Consider slight undercutting of competitors for price-sensitive buyers, if feasible.

5. Pricing Flexibility:
   - Seasonal Adjustments: Adapt pricing to seasonal demands or market fluctuations.

Price Testing: Experiment with different price points to assess buyer response and optimize strategies.

6. Balancing Price and Quality:

Avoiding Overpricing: Ensure prices align with item condition, features, and competitive landscape.

Emphasizing Value: Highlight quality, uniqueness, and benefits in descriptions to support the price.

7. Promotions and Discounts:

Strategic Offerings: Use eBay's promotional tools for discounts, specials, or limited-time offers.

Bulk Deals or Bundles: Offer discounts on multiple purchases or appealing bundles for added value.

8. Continuous Monitoring and Adaptation:

Performance Analysis: Regularly monitor sales, adjust pricing based on analytics, and identify trends.

Adapting to Market: Adjust pricing strategies to changing conditions, buyer preferences, and competitor actions.

9. Compliance and Transparency:

Adherence to Policies: Ensure prices align with eBay regulations, avoiding price manipulation.

Transparent Communication: Clearly communicate prices, shipping costs, and additional charges for buyer trust.

Using High-Quality Images

Importance of High-Quality Images:

Visual Appeal: High-quality images capture attention and entice potential buyers, increasing listing visibility.

Enhanced Perception: Clear, detailed images convey professionalism, build trust, and showcase the product accurately.

Image Standards and Requirements:

Resolution and Size: eBay recommends images of at least 500 pixels on the longest side, enabling zoom and clear visibility.

File Format: Use JPEG, PNG, or GIF formats for optimum compatibility and quality.

Image Composition and Presentation:

Multiple Angles: Include shots from various angles to offer a comprehensive view of the product's features and condition.

Close-Ups and Details: Showcase intricate details, textures, and any flaws transparently for buyer confidence.

Lighting and Background:

Optimal Lighting: Use natural light or soft artificial lighting to highlight details and avoid harsh shadows or glare.

Neutral Background: Utilize plain backgrounds to focus on the item, ensuring it stands out without distractions.

Consistency and Accuracy:

Consistent Style: Maintain a consistent image style and size throughout listings for a professional appearance.

Accurate Representation: Ensure images accurately represent the item's color, size, and condition to prevent buyer dissatisfaction.

Professional Photography Tips:

Staging and Props: Consider using props or staging to showcase the product in use or its scale for better context.

Editing and Retouching: Edit images for brightness, contrast, and sharpness, avoiding excessive manipulation.

Image Quantity and Variety:

Include Multiple Images: Provide the maximum allowable images to cover all product aspects comprehensively.

Infographics or Charts: Use infographics or comparison charts for technical specifications or size measurements.

Mobile Optimization:

Mobile-Friendly Images: Ensure images are clear and easily viewable on mobile devices, catering to a diverse audience.

Branding and Watermarks:

Subtle Branding: Consider subtle watermarks or branding to protect images while maintaining focus on the product.

Placement Consideration: Place watermarks strategically to prevent obstruction of key product details.

Testing and Optimization:

A/B Testing: Experiment with image variations to identify which styles or angles resonate best with buyers.

Performance Analysis: Analyze listing performance based on image quality and adjust strategies accordingly.

CHAPTER THREE

Effective Selling Strategies

Navigating the vast landscape of selling strategies on platforms like eBay requires a tailored approach. Effective selling hinges on a deliberate selection of strategies that align with your goals, product offerings, and market dynamics. This journey involves identifying the most impactful methods—from pricing strategies to customer service approaches—that resonate with your audience and optimize your sales. Let's explore the essential considerations and diverse tactics available to craft a winning selling strategy tailored to your unique seller profile.

Auctions vs. Buy-It-Now: Choosing the Right Format

Choosing between auction and buy-it-now formats on platforms like eBay is a critical decision that impacts sales strategies and buyer engagement. It requires a careful assessment of product type, market demand, and seller objectives. Each format offers distinct advantages, and leveraging the right strategy at the right time can significantly impact sales success on platforms like eBay. Here's a comprehensive guide to help navigate this choice enabling them to optimize their sales strategies effectively.

Choosing the Right Selling Format: Auction vs. Buy-It-Now

1. Auction Format:

Dynamic Pricing: Allows bidding where buyers compete, potentially increasing the final sale price.

Engagement and Urgency: Generates excitement and urgency, attracting buyers who enjoy the bidding process.

Unique or Rare Items: Ideal for unique, collectible, or niche products with uncertain market values.

2. Buy-It-Now Format:

Fixed Price Selling: Offers a stable, predictable price, suitable for immediate purchase without bidding.

Convenience and Instant Sale: Attracts buyers seeking immediate gratification or specific items.

Brand New or High Demand: Suitable for new or high-demand items with clear market values.

Factors Influencing the Decision:

Item Type and Demand:

Scarcity and Uniqueness: Rare or collectible items often perform well in auctions due to their uniqueness.

Brand New or Common Items: Common or readily available products often sell better with a fixed buy-it-now price.

Seller Preferences and Objectives:

Quick Turnaround: Buy-it-now offers immediate sales, whereas auctions might take longer but potentially yield higher prices.

Control Over Pricing: Auctions allow for dynamic pricing, but buy-it-now offers control over fixed prices.

Buyer Behavior and Market Trends:

Buyer Preference: Consider the preferences of your target audience—some prefer the excitement of auctions while others favor instant purchases.

Market Trends: Analyze market trends to understand what format is more popular for similar products.

Optimizing Strategies for Each Format:

Auction Format:

Strategic Timing: Optimal listing durations and ending times to maximize bidding activity.

Starting Prices: Consider setting attractive starting prices to encourage bidding wars.

Detailed Descriptions: Provide comprehensive details to attract and engage potential bidders.

Buy-It-Now Format:

Competitive Pricing: Research and set competitive, yet profitable, fixed prices.

Quality Images and Descriptions: High-quality images and detailed descriptions are crucial for immediate buyer decisions.

Offer Combined Shipping or Deals: Incentivize buyers with combined shipping or promotional deals.

Utilizing Best Practices for Product Listings

Crafting compelling and effective product listings is a strategic art that can significantly impact sales and buyer engagement on platforms like eBay. By employing best practices, sellers can enhance the visibility, attractiveness, and credibility of their listings. From attention-grabbing titles to informative descriptions, high-quality images, and competitive pricing, utilizing these practices optimizes listings, capturing the interest of potential buyers and fostering successful transactions. Let's explore the key strategies and techniques that elevate product listings to drive sales and create a positive buyer experience.

1. Compelling Titles:

- Keyword-Rich Titles: Craft concise, descriptive titles with relevant keywords to enhance search visibility.
- Highlight Key Features: Include essential details like brand, model, size, color, and unique selling points.

2. Detailed Descriptions:

Informative Content: Provide comprehensive yet concise descriptions covering product specifications, condition, and benefits.

Use Bullet Points: Organize details using bullet points for easy readability and quick comprehension.

3. High-Quality Images:

Multiple Angles: Showcase products from various angles to provide a complete view.

Clear and Detailed: Use high-resolution images to display product features and textures accurately.

4. Accurate Item Specifics:

Fill Item Details: Input accurate item specifics like size, material, condition, and compatibility to aid search accuracy.

Utilize eBay's Fields: Make use of eBay's provided fields to include relevant specifics about the item.

5. Competitive Pricing:

Value-Based Pricing: Set prices competitively, aligning with market trends and the product's value.

Strategic Discounting: Offer occasional discounts or bundle deals to attract buyers.

6. Shipping and Returns Information:

Clear Policies: Define shipping costs, handling times, and return policies clearly to enhance buyer confidence.

Fast and Reliable Shipping: Ensure prompt shipping and reliable delivery to foster positive buyer experiences.

7. Optimize Keywords and SEO:

Keyword Research: Utilize relevant keywords in titles and descriptions for improved search ranking.

SEO-Friendly Content: Write content that appeals to search algorithms without compromising readability.

8. Professionalism and Branding:

- Consistent Branding: Maintain a consistent tone and visual style across listings to establish a professional brand image.
- Use Templates or Themes: Employ templates or themes to maintain consistency and professionalism.

9. Customer Engagement and Communication:

- Prompt Responses: Respond quickly to buyer inquiries and maintain clear communication throughout the transaction process.
- Address Buyer Concerns: Be transparent and address buyer queries promptly and professionally.

10. Analyze and Iterate:

- Performance Evaluation: Regularly analyze listing performance metrics such as views, conversions, and sales.
- Iterative Improvement: Based on analytics, refine listings, experiment with different strategies, and adapt to market trends.

11. Compliance and Ethics:

- Adherence to eBay Policies: Ensure compliance with eBay's listing policies, avoiding prohibited content or deceptive practices.
- Ethical Representations: Provide accurate and truthful information about the item, avoiding misleading descriptions.

12. Mobile Optimization:

- Mobile-Friendly Listings: Ensure listings are mobile-responsive for seamless user experience across devices.

Managing Inventory and Shipping

Efficiently managing inventory and shipping processes is pivotal for successful e-commerce operations. From maintaining accurate stock levels to ensuring timely deliveries, effective management streamlines operations, enhances customer satisfaction, and drives business growth. The following are guides to mastering inventory control and optimizing shipping logistics for seamless transactions and satisfied customers.

Inventory Management:

a. Inventory Tracking:

Real-time Monitoring: Employ inventory management software for accurate, real-time tracking of stock levels.

Regular Audits: Conduct routine audits to reconcile physical inventory with digital records, minimizing discrepancies.

b. Forecasting and Replenishment:

Demand Forecasting: Utilize historical data and market trends to forecast demand and plan inventory restocking.

Reorder Points: Set reorder points to ensure timely restocking and prevent stockouts or overstocking.

c. Organized Warehouse Management:

Optimized Layout: Organize the warehouse for efficient picking, packing, and restocking processes.

Labeling and Categorization: Implement clear labeling and categorization to locate items swiftly and reduce errors.

Shipping Logistics:

a. Shipping Strategy:

Carrier Selection: Choose reliable carriers based on cost, reliability, and delivery speed for various destinations.

Shipping Options: Offer multiple shipping options to cater to diverse buyer preferences and urgency levels.

b. Packaging and Handling:

- Secure Packaging: Ensure products are securely packaged to prevent damage during transit.
- Efficient Handling: Streamline packing processes to minimize handling time and errors in order fulfillment.

c. Tracking and Customer Communication:

- Shipment Tracking: Provide customers with tracking information for transparency and peace of mind.
- Proactive Communication: Notify buyers promptly about shipping updates or delays for exceptional customer service.

Returns and Reverse Logistics:

a. Returns Management:

- Clear Return Policies: Establish clear and user-friendly return policies to ease the return process for customers.
- Efficient Handling: Streamline the return process to promptly assess, restock, or refund returned items.

b. Reverse Logistics Optimization:

- Refurbishment or Resale: Evaluate returned items for refurbishment, resale, or efficient disposal to minimize losses.
- Feedback Integration: Incorporate returned product feedback into inventory management and product improvement strategies.

Technology Integration and Automation:

a. Inventory Software Integration:

- Automation Tools: Integrate inventory software for automated stock updates, order processing, and forecasting.
- Barcode/RFID Systems: Implement barcode or RFID systems for accurate inventory tracking and management.

b. Shipping Automation:

Label Printing Systems: Use label printing systems to automate shipping label creation, reducing manual errors.

Order Fulfillment Platforms: Utilize order fulfillment platforms for streamlined shipping and tracking.

Continuous Improvement and Analysis:

a. Performance Metrics:

Analytical Insights: Use performance metrics like order processing times, delivery accuracy, and customer feedback for continuous improvement.

Adapting Strategies: Adjust inventory and shipping strategies based on data insights and market fluctuations.

b. Process Optimization:

Iterative Enhancements: Continuously refine inventory and shipping processes for efficiency and cost-effectiveness.

Adaptability: Stay agile and adaptable to changes in customer demands, technology, and logistics trends.

CHAPTER FOUR

Maximizing Visibility and Sales

Maximizing visibility and sales on eBay demands a multi-faceted approach that integrates optimized listings, competitive pricing, effective use of eBay's tools, SEO strategies, exemplary customer service, and continuous improvement based on data-driven insights. By implementing these strategic tactics, sellers can enhance visibility, attract more buyers, and ultimately drive sales growth in the dynamic online marketplace.

1. Optimize Product Listings:

a. Compelling Titles and Descriptions:

Craft keyword-rich titles and detailed descriptions to enhance search visibility.
Highlight key features, benefits, and unique selling points to attract buyers.

b. High-Quality Images:

Utilize high-resolution images from multiple angles to showcase products accurately.
Ensure clear, professional visuals to captivate potential buyers.

2. Strategic Pricing Strategies:

a. Competitive Pricing:

Research market trends and competitors to set competitive yet profitable prices.
Consider occasional discounts or promotional pricing to attract buyers.

b. Auction vs. Buy-It-Now:

Choose between auction or fixed-price formats based on product uniqueness, demand, and buyer behavior.

3. Utilize eBay's Tools and Features:

a. Promotions and Discounts:

Leverage eBay's promotional tools to offer discounts, bundle deals, or seasonal sales.
Utilize markdown manager or sales events for increased visibility.

b. Sponsored Listings and Advertising:

Invest in sponsored listings or advertising to boost visibility for specific products.
Target relevant keywords and categories for increased exposure.

4. Optimize SEO and Keywords:

a. Keyword Optimization:

Research and include relevant keywords in titles and descriptions for better search rankings.
Use eBay's search bar and analytics to identify popular search terms.

b. SEO-Friendly Content:

Write content that appeals to search algorithms without compromising readability.
Use structured data and HTML tags effectively for improved search indexing.

5. Provide Exceptional Customer Service:

a. Fast and Transparent Communication:

Respond promptly to buyer inquiries and maintain clear, professional communication.
Address buyer concerns and provide timely updates on orders and shipments.

b. Positive Feedback and Reviews:

Encourage buyers to leave positive feedback through exceptional service and accurate product descriptions.
Maintain transparency and resolve issues promptly to foster positive reviews.

6. Mobile Optimization:

a. Mobile-Friendly Listings:

Ensure listings are mobile-responsive for easy access and navigation on various devices.
Optimize images and content for seamless mobile viewing.

b. eBay App Integration:

Leverage eBay's mobile app features for quick updates, communication, and managing listings on the go.

7. Continuous Analysis and Improvement:

a. Performance Metrics Evaluation:

Regularly analyze sales metrics, conversion rates, and traffic to optimize strategies.

Use eBay analytics and tools to measure performance and identify areas for improvement.

b. Adaptation to Market Changes:

Stay updated on market trends, eBay policies, and customer preferences to adapt strategies proactively.
Experiment with different tactics and adapt based on data insights and customer feedback.

Enhancing Listings with Keywords and SEO

Keyword Research:

a. eBay's Search Bar:

Utilize eBay's search bar to discover popular search terms related to your product.
Analyze auto-suggestions for keyword ideas that buyers commonly use.
b. External Tools:

Use third-party keyword research tools to identify high-ranking keywords relevant to your product.
Consider long-tail keywords specific to your item for niche targeting.

Optimizing Title and Description:

a. Title Optimization:

Craft descriptive titles containing relevant keywords to improve search visibility.

Prioritize key details like brand, model, size, color, and unique selling points within the character limit.

b. Description Enhancement:

Incorporate chosen keywords naturally throughout the description for SEO optimization.

Create informative, detailed, and keyword-rich descriptions, offering value to potential buyers.

Item Specifics and Categories:

a. Detailed Item Specifics:

Fill in all available item specifics accurately, using relevant keywords to enhance search accuracy.

eBay's structured data fields allow you to input essential details, optimizing search visibility.

b. Selecting Categories:

Choose the most relevant category and subcategories for your product to reach the right audience.

eBay's category system aids in better search placement and visibility.

Visual Content Optimization:

a. Image File Names and Alt Tags:

Rename image files using descriptive keywords before uploading them.

Utilize alt tags with descriptive text to optimize images for search engines.

b. Image Captions and Descriptions:

Add captions or descriptions to images with relevant keywords for additional SEO benefits.

Ensure images are high-quality, showcasing product details from various angles.

eBay Store Optimization:

a. Storefront SEO:

Optimize your eBay store's title, description, and about us section with relevant keywords.
Use SEO-friendly store categories and pages for better navigation and search ranking.
b. Cross-Promotion Strategies:

Cross-promote related items within your store to encourage additional sales and increase visibility.
Employ featured listings or promotional slots within your store for highlighted items.

Monitoring and Adaptation:

a. Analyzing Performance:

Regularly review eBay analytics to track the performance of your listings and SEO efforts.
Monitor keyword effectiveness, traffic sources, and conversion rates for continual improvement.
b. A/B Testing and Iteration:

Conduct A/B tests by experimenting with different keywords, titles, or descriptions.
Adapt strategies based on data insights, optimizing listings for better search rankings and conversions.

Compliance and Ethics:

a. Adherence to eBay Policies:

Ensure compliance with eBay's policies, avoiding keyword stuffing or misleading practices.
Maintain honesty and accuracy in listings, adhering to eBay's guidelines and regulations.
b. Ethical Representation:

Provide genuine and accurate information, avoiding manipulative tactics or false claims in listings.

Implementing these comprehensive keyword strategies and SEO techniques in eBay listings is fundamental to increasing visibility, attracting relevant traffic, and driving sales.

Utilizing Promotions and Discounts

1. Promotion Types and Tools:

a. Markdown Manager:
- Utilize eBay's Markdown Manager to create temporary discounts, sales, or clearance events.
- Set percentage or fixed-price discounts on selected items to attract buyers and increase visibility.

b. Volume Pricing and Bundling:
- Offer discounts for bulk purchases or create bundle deals to incentivize larger orders.
- Set tiered pricing or bundle packages to encourage multiple purchases from buyers.

2. Promotional Campaign Strategies:

a. Seasonal Sales and Events:
- Plan and schedule promotions around seasonal events, holidays, or special occasions.
- Offer themed discounts or limited-time offers to capitalize on increased buyer interest.

b. Flash Sales and Limited-Time Offers:
- Create urgency by running flash sales or time-sensitive promotions to prompt immediate purchases.
- Employ countdown timers or promotional banners for increased visibility and urgency.

3. Featured Listings and Visibility:

a. eBay's Promoted Listings:
- Invest in eBay's promoted listings to boost visibility by showcasing your items in prominent spots.
- Pay for increased exposure, appearing prominently in search results for selected keywords.

b. Home Page and Category Features:
- Utilize eBay's home page or category features to showcase discounted or promoted items.
- Featured listings gain additional visibility, increasing the likelihood of attracting buyers.

4. Communication and Marketing:

a. Email Marketing and Newsletter Integration:
- Integrate promotions in newsletters or email campaigns to reach out to existing and potential buyers.
- Highlight ongoing sales, discounts, or exclusive offers to encourage purchases.

b. Social Media Promotion:

- Share promotional campaigns across social media platforms to expand reach and attract new buyers.
- Leverage social media channels to create buzz and drive traffic to discounted items on eBay.

5. Monitoring and Optimization:
a. Performance Analysis:
- Regularly analyze the performance of promotional campaigns using eBay's analytics tools.
- Monitor sales metrics, conversion rates, and traffic sources to measure the effectiveness of promotions.

b. Iterative Improvement:
- Adapt strategies based on data insights, tweaking discounts, timing, or promotion types for better results.
- Test different promotional tactics and optimize based on what resonates best with your audience.

Conclusion: Driving Sales through Strategic Promotions

Effectively utilizing promotions and discounts on eBay is a powerful strategy to increase visibility, attract buyers, and drive sales. By leveraging various promotional tools, planning strategic campaigns, enhancing visibility through featured listings, and continuously analyzing and optimizing promotional efforts, sellers can significantly enhance their reach, engage potential buyers, and stimulate sales growth in the competitive eBay marketplace.

Leveraging eBay's Marketing Tools

1. Promoted Listings:

Increased Visibility: Use Promoted Listings to showcase items prominently in search results, category pages, and more.
Cost-Per-Sale Model: Pay only when a sale occurs from a promoted item, maximizing ROI.
Flexible Budgeting: Set budgets and ad rates based on individual item goals and profit margins.

2. eBay Stores:

Custom Storefront: Utilize eBay Stores to create a branded, customizable storefront showcasing your products.
Subscription Benefits: Subscribers gain access to additional marketing tools, customizable templates, and promotional features.

3. Promotional Sales Events:

Markdown Manager: Create temporary discounts, sales, or clearance events using Markdown Manager.
Volume Pricing: Offer discounts for bulk purchases or create bundle deals to incentivize larger orders.

4. Featured Listings:

Home Page and Category Features: Utilize eBay's home page or category features to highlight discounted or promoted items.
Increased Visibility: Featured listings attract more attention, leading to higher visibility and potential sales.

5. Email Marketing Integration:

Customer Communication: Integrate promotions and offers into email campaigns to reach existing and potential buyers.
Exclusive Deals: Share exclusive discounts or special offers via email to encourage purchases.

6. Social Media Integration:

Expanded Reach: Share promotional campaigns across social media platforms to attract new buyers.
Engagement Tactics: Use social media channels to engage buyers and drive traffic to eBay listings.

7. eBay's Analytics and Insights:

Performance Tracking: Regularly monitor sales metrics, conversion rates, and traffic sources using eBay's analytics tools.
Data-Driven Decisions: Utilize insights to optimize marketing strategies and make informed decisions.

8. Sponsored Listings:

Boosted Visibility: Invest in Sponsored Listings to increase visibility for specific products in search results.
Cost Control: Set maximum CPC (Cost Per Click) bids to manage advertising spend effectively.

9. Seasonal Campaigns:

Holiday or Event-Specific Offers: Plan and schedule promotions around key holidays or events.
Tailored Promotions: Create themed promotions aligned with seasonal trends to attract seasonal buyers.

10. Continuous Optimization:

A/B Testing: Experiment with different marketing tactics, keywords, or promotional offers to determine what resonates best.
Adaptation and Improvement: Continuously adapt strategies based on performance metrics and market trends.

CHAPTER FIVE

Providing Excellent Customer Service

Providing outstanding customer service on eBay is pivotal for fostering positive buyer experiences and establishing a strong seller reputation within the online marketplace. By implementing strategic practices and maintaining a customer-centric approach, sellers can elevate their service standards, build trust, and encourage repeat business.

1. Communication Excellence:

Timely and effective communication is the cornerstone of exceptional customer service. Responding promptly to buyer inquiries, messages, and concerns within eBay's messaging system demonstrates attentiveness and a commitment to buyer satisfaction. Maintaining a professional tone and clarity in all interactions helps build rapport and trust with customers.

2. Detailed and Transparent Listings:

Accurate and comprehensive item descriptions are imperative. Providing detailed information about products, including specifications, condition, and features, accompanied by high-quality images from various angles, enhances transparency and helps manage buyer expectations. Clearly outlining shipping, return, and refund policies within each listing fosters trust and reduces misunderstandings.

3. Efficient Order Fulfillment:

Fast and reliable order processing and shipping are essential for positive buyer experiences. Adhering to stated handling times and promptly shipping items while ensuring secure packaging helps maintain buyer confidence. Providing tracking information allows buyers to monitor their shipments, enhancing transparency and reliability.

4. Addressing Buyer Concerns Proactively:

Handling returns, refunds, or exchanges promptly and professionally is crucial. Adhering to eBay's return policies and resolving disputes in a fair and amicable manner showcases dedication to buyer satisfaction. Effectively managing negative feedback by addressing issues constructively demonstrates commitment to improving services and rectifying any shortcomings.

5. Engaging Proactively with Customers:

Following up after a sale to ensure buyer satisfaction and encouraging feedback or reviews helps maintain open lines of communication. Offering incentives or loyalty programs for repeat purchases encourages customer loyalty and showcases appreciation for their business.

6. Leveraging eBay's Tools for Resolution:

Utilizing eBay's messaging system for all buyer-seller communications and resolving disputes through the Resolution Center showcases professionalism and adherence to eBay's policies. Striving for amicable resolutions in cases of disputes fosters positive buyer-seller relationships.

7. Consistency and Continuous Improvement:

Consistent service standards across all transactions, maintaining reliability in shipping times, item quality, and customer support, build buyer trust. Regularly analyzing feedback, adapting to market changes, and continuously improving services based on insights gleaned from buyer interactions are vital for ongoing enhancement.

In Conclusion: Elevating Buyer Experiences for Long-Term Success
Exceptional customer service on eBay involves proactive communication, transparency, efficient order processing, proactive engagement, effective issue resolution, and a commitment to continuous improvement. By

prioritizing buyer satisfaction and consistently delivering outstanding service, sellers not only build a loyal customer base but also elevate their reputation and success within the competitive eBay marketplace.

Establishing Trust with Buyers

Establishing trust with buyers is fundamental for successful transactions and fostering long-term relationships within the eBay marketplace. By implementing trust-building strategies and demonstrating reliability and transparency, sellers can instill confidence and create positive buyer experiences.

Creating listings that are accurate, detailed, and transparent is key. Providing comprehensive information about products, including clear descriptions, specifications, and condition, alongside high-quality images, builds buyer confidence. Transparently disclosing any imperfections or wear in used items helps manage buyer expectations and avoids misunderstandings.

Timely and transparent communication is crucial for fostering trust. Responding promptly to buyer inquiries, messages, and concerns showcases attentiveness and reliability. Maintaining a professional tone and providing clear and concise information in all communications reinforces trust in the seller.

Consistency in order processing and shipping is vital. Adhering to stated handling times, promptly shipping items, and ensuring secure packaging conveys reliability and professionalism. Providing accurate tracking information allows buyers to track their shipments, reinforcing confidence in the seller.

Being honest and transparent in all transactions builds credibility. Clearly outlining shipping, return, and refund policies within listings helps set clear expectations for buyers. Honoring these policies consistently and ethically resolves any issues that may arise, reinforcing trust in the seller's integrity.

Handling any buyer concerns or issues promptly and professionally is essential. Resolving disputes or addressing problems in a fair and amicable manner demonstrates commitment to buyer satisfaction. Transparently communicating throughout the resolution process reinforces trust and reliability.

Consistency in service standards, shipping times, and product quality is crucial. Maintaining reliability in all transactions and consistently delivering as promised reinforces the seller's trustworthiness. Upholding these standards consistently fosters positive buyer-seller relationships.

Seeking feedback and actively incorporating suggestions for improvement demonstrates a commitment to enhancing services. Regularly analyzing buyer feedback and adapting based on insights gleaned from buyer interactions are crucial for continual improvement and reinforcing trust.

Building trust with buyers on eBay involves transparent and accurate listings, reliable communication, consistent order fulfillment, honesty in transactions, proactive issue resolution, and a commitment to continuous improvement. By prioritizing transparency, reliability, and ethical practices, sellers not only establish trust but also cultivate lasting relationships and credibility within the eBay community.

Handling Inquiries and Resolving Issues

Providing exceptional customer service on eBay involves adeptly managing inquiries and swiftly resolving any issues that may arise during buyer interactions. Effectively handling these aspects not only ensures positive experiences but also nurtures trust and credibility with buyers, fostering strong relationships within the online marketplace.

1. Prompt and Professional Communication:

Timely responses to buyer inquiries are pivotal. Ensuring prompt communication within eBay's messaging system exhibits attentiveness and commitment. Maintaining a professional and courteous tone in all interactions fosters positive rapport and enhances the buyer's experience.

2. Detailed and Transparent Information:

Accurate and detailed product descriptions are key. Providing comprehensive information about items, including specifications, condition, and relevant details, alongside high-quality images, reinforces transparency and manages buyer expectations effectively.

3. Clear Policy Outlines:

Transparency in policies is crucial. Clearly outlining shipping, return, and refund policies within listings aids in setting clear expectations for buyers. Adhering consistently to these policies builds trust and minimizes misunderstandings.

4. Proactive Issue Resolution:

Addressing buyer concerns promptly is vital. Resolving issues or disputes professionally and in a timely manner demonstrates commitment to buyer satisfaction. Striving for fair resolutions within eBay guidelines fosters positive buyer-seller relationships.

5. Efficient Handling of Returns and Refunds:

Adhering diligently to eBay's return and refund policies streamlines issue resolution. Processing returns and refunds promptly upon receiving returned items ensures a seamless experience for buyers.

6. Utilization of eBay's Communication Tools:
Leveraging eBay's messaging system for all buyer-seller communications maintains a centralized and effective channel. Utilizing the Resolution Center to manage and address disputes or issues reinforces professionalism and adherence to eBay's policies.

7. Building Trust through Proactive Engagement:
Maintaining open lines of communication and proactive follow-up after issue resolution fosters positive relationships. Seeking feedback and adapting practices based on buyer insights demonstrate dedication to improvement and customer satisfaction.

8. Continuous Improvement and Consistency:
Analyzing buyer feedback and adapting strategies for ongoing improvement is crucial. Consistency in service standards, such as reliable shipping times and adherence to policies, solidifies buyer trust and confidence in the seller.

Managing Feedback and Reviews

Feedback and reviews on eBay play a pivotal role in shaping a seller's reputation and influencing buyer confidence. Effectively managing feedback, encouraging positive reviews, and addressing concerns are vital for maintaining a positive seller profile and fostering trust within the eBay community.

1. Encouraging Positive Feedback:

- Prompt Order Fulfillment: Ensure timely shipping and delivery of items to buyers.

- Quality Products and Service: Provide excellent service and high-quality products to prompt positive feedback.
- Proactive Communication: Engage with buyers, resolve issues promptly, and seek positive feedback upon successful transactions.

2. Responding to Feedback Professionally:

- Acknowledging Positive Feedback: Thank buyers for positive feedback to reinforce appreciation for their support.
- Addressing Negative Feedback: Respond courteously and professionally to negative feedback, offering resolutions or explanations publicly while seeking a resolution privately.

3. Proactive Issue Resolution:

- Addressing Buyer Concerns: Promptly address any buyer concerns or issues raised through feedback or reviews.
- Resolving Disputes Amicably: Strive for fair and amicable solutions within eBay's guidelines to rectify any reported issues.

4. Seeking Constructive Feedback:

- Feedback Request: Encourage buyers to leave feedback and reviews upon successful transactions.
- Feedback Analysis: Analyze feedback trends to identify areas for improvement and adapt practices for better customer satisfaction.

5. Maintaining Transparency and Honesty:

- Accurate Representation: Ensure listings are accurate and transparent to manage buyer expectations.
- Ethical Practices: Maintain honesty in all transactions and adhere to eBay policies for transparent dealings.

6. Leveraging Positive Reviews:

- Showcasing Positive Feedback: Highlight positive reviews in product listings or seller profiles to bolster credibility.
- Building Trust: Utilize positive feedback to build buyer confidence and trust in the seller's reputation.

7. Continuous Improvement and Adaptation:

- Feedback Integration: Continuously integrate feedback insights to enhance services and refine business practices.
- Adapting to Buyer Expectations: Adapt strategies based on feedback to meet changing buyer preferences and expectations.

8. Consistency in Service Excellence:

- Reliable Service Standards: Maintain consistency in providing reliable service, shipping times, and product quality.
- Building Credibility: Consistent service builds credibility and reinforces buyer trust in the seller.

CHAPTER SIX

Managing Your eBay Business

Managing an eBay account involves a series of tasks aimed at optimizing sales, maintaining a positive reputation, and fostering a seamless buying and selling experience. From overseeing listings to maintaining customer relations, various elements contribute to successful account management on eBay.

1. Account Dashboard Navigation:

Understanding eBay's Interface: Familiarize yourself with the eBay dashboard, which serves as the centralized hub for account management.
Navigation and Tools: Explore different sections like "My eBay," "Seller Hub," and "Account Settings" to access key tools for managing listings, orders, and account preferences.

2. Listing Management:

Creating Listings: Utilize eBay's listing tools to create accurate, detailed, and attractive listings with clear descriptions and quality images.
Monitoring and Updating: Regularly monitor active listings, update inventory, and revise listings based on performance metrics or buyer feedback.

3. Pricing Strategies:

Competitive Pricing: Set competitive prices based on market trends, competitor analysis, and the item's condition and demand.
Utilizing eBay Tools: Utilize eBay's pricing tools like auction-style or fixed-price listings to optimize sales based on item types.

4. Order Processing and Fulfillment:

Timely Order Fulfillment: Process orders promptly, adhere to stated handling times, and ensure secure packaging for safe delivery.
Shipping and Tracking: Provide accurate shipping information and tracking details to buyers for transparency.

5. Customer Communication:

Prompt Responses: Respond promptly to buyer inquiries, messages, and concerns within eBay's messaging system.
Professional Communication: Maintain a professional and courteous tone in all interactions, addressing buyer concerns or issues promptly.

6. Feedback and Review Management:

Encouraging Positive Feedback: Provide excellent service to encourage positive feedback from buyers upon successful transactions.
Addressing Negative Feedback: Respond courteously and professionally to negative feedback, seeking resolutions publicly and privately.

7. Utilizing eBay's Seller Tools:

Seller Hub and Analytics: Utilize eBay's Seller Hub to access performance metrics, sales reports, and seller tools for data-driven decision-making.
Marketing and Promotions: Make use of eBay's marketing tools like Promoted Listings to increase visibility and sales.

8. Compliance and Policy Adherence:

Adhering to eBay Policies: Ensure compliance with eBay's policies, including listing guidelines, payment procedures, and seller standards.
Ethical Practices: Maintain ethical and transparent practices in all transactions to build trust with buyers and eBay.

9. Continuous Improvement and Learning:

Feedback Analysis: Analyze buyer feedback and sales performance to identify areas for improvement.
Adapting Strategies: Continuously adapt strategies based on data insights, market trends, and customer preferences.

10. Security and Account Maintenance:

Account Security: Ensure strong passwords, enable two-factor authentication, and regularly update account information for security.
Maintenance and Review: Regularly review account settings, update policies, and adjust preferences as needed.

Monitoring Sales and Analytics

Monitoring sales and analyzing analytics on eBay provides sellers with invaluable insights for informed decision-making and strategy optimization. By leveraging eBay's analytics tools, understanding buyer behavior, adapting strategies based on performance metrics, and continually striving for improvement, sellers can drive success, maximize sales, and maintain a competitive edge within the dynamic eBay marketplace.

1. Utilizing eBay's Seller Hub:

- Access to Performance Metrics: Navigate through eBay's Seller Hub to access comprehensive performance metrics and analytics.
- Overview of Sales Data: Review detailed reports on sales, traffic, and customer behavior to gauge overall performance.

2. Sales Performance Analysis:

- Track Sales Trends: Monitor sales trends, including revenue, units sold, average selling price, and fluctuations over specific periods.
- Comparative Analysis: Analyze sales performance across different products, categories, or time frames to identify top-performing items.

3. Traffic Sources and Conversion Rates:

- Understanding Traffic Sources: Analyze traffic sources, such as direct searches, promotions, or external referrals, to understand where buyers are coming from.
- Conversion Rate Analysis: Measure conversion rates to evaluate the effectiveness of listings in converting views into sales.

4. Customer Behavior Insights:

- Buyer Engagement: Assess buyer behavior metrics like click-through rates, watch counts, and time spent on listings to understand buyer interest.
- Repeat Buyer Analysis: Track repeat purchases or customer retention to gauge satisfaction and loyalty.

5. Inventory and Listing Analysis:

- Inventory Performance: Evaluate inventory turnover rates, assess slow-moving items, and manage stock levels based on demand and performance.
- Listing Performance Review: Analyze individual listing performance, identifying high-performing listings and optimizing low-performing ones.

6. eBay's Analytics Tools:

- Terapeak Research: Use eBay's Terapeak tool for market research, competitive analysis, and trend identification.
- Data-Driven Decisions: Utilize data insights to adjust pricing, optimize listing details, and tailor marketing strategies.

7. Adapting Strategies Based on Insights:

- Optimization of Listings: Adjust titles, descriptions, or images based on analytics to improve visibility and conversion rates.
- Pricing Strategies: Modify pricing strategies or introduce promotions based on sales performance and market trends.

8. Seasonal and Trend Analysis:

- Seasonal Trends Identification: Identify and capitalize on seasonal trends or events to adjust inventory and marketing strategies.
- Market Trend Awareness: Stay updated on market trends, consumer preferences, and competitor activities to adapt strategies proactively.

9. Performance Goals and Assessments:

- Setting Performance Benchmarks: Establish measurable goals based on analytics to track progress and success.
- Regular Assessments: Conduct periodic reviews and assessments to ensure strategies align with performance objectives.

10. Continuous Learning and Improvement:

- Adapting to Changes: Stay agile and flexible, adapting strategies based on changing market dynamics and customer behavior.
- Feedback Integration: Incorporate feedback from analytics to refine listings, improve customer service, and enhance overall performance.

Scaling Your eBay Business

Expanding and scaling a business on eBay requires a multifaceted approach that integrates effective strategies, optimized operations, and leveraging the platform's features to achieve sustained growth and success.

1. Optimize Listings and Product Range:

Diversify Product Portfolio: Expand your product range strategically to attract a wider customer base.

Optimized Listings: Ensure compelling and SEO-friendly listings with high-quality images and detailed descriptions to increase visibility and sales potential.

Utilize eBay's Catalog: Leverage eBay's catalog feature to align with standardized product information, enhancing discoverability.

2. Pricing Strategies and Competitive Positioning:

Dynamic Pricing: Implement competitive pricing strategies, considering market trends, competitor analysis, and buyer demand.

Value Proposition: Highlight unique selling points to differentiate products and maintain a competitive edge.

Consideration of Fees: Factor in eBay fees and expenses while setting competitive prices for profitability.

3. Efficient Inventory Management:

Inventory Analysis: Continuously analyze inventory performance, identifying fast-moving and slow-moving items to optimize stock levels.

Supplier Relationships: Strengthen relationships with suppliers for competitive pricing, reliability, and streamlined supply chains.

4. Strategic Marketing and Promotions:

- Promoted Listings: Utilize eBay's Promoted Listings feature to boost visibility for key products, reaching a broader audience.
- Targeted Campaigns: Implement targeted marketing campaigns during peak seasons or special events to capitalize on increased buyer activity.

5. Customer Service Excellence:

- Enhanced Support: Maintain high-quality customer service with prompt responses to inquiries, efficient issue resolution, and proactive communication.
- Feedback Management: Encourage positive feedback and actively address negative feedback to enhance seller reputation.

6. Seller Performance and Standards:

- Maintain High Standards: Comply with eBay's seller standards to ensure consistent performance and sustain a top-rated seller status.
- Continuous Improvement: Adapt strategies based on performance metrics and buyer feedback for ongoing improvement.

7. Utilize eBay's Seller Tools:

- Seller Hub and Analytics: Leverage eBay's Seller Hub and analytics tools for comprehensive insights into sales performance, trends, and buyer behavior.
- Integration of Marketing Tools: Make effective use of eBay's marketing tools, such as promotions, discounts, and sponsored listings, to enhance visibility and sales.

8. Expansion into International Markets:

- Global Selling: Explore international expansion by leveraging eBay's global platform to reach a broader customer base.
- Localization Strategies: Tailor listings and marketing efforts to suit regional preferences and cultural nuances for better market penetration.

9. Streamline Operations and Efficiency:

- Automation and Streamlining: Implement tools or software to automate repetitive tasks, streamline order processing, and enhance operational efficiency.
- Outsourcing Consideration: Consider outsourcing certain tasks, such as shipping and customer service, for scalability.

10. Continuous Evaluation and Adaptation:

- Regular Assessment: Continuously assess performance metrics, sales trends, and market shifts to adapt strategies for ongoing growth.
- Agile Adaptation: Remain flexible and agile in response to changing market dynamics, technology advancements, and buyer behavior.

Staying Compliant with eBay Policies

eBay, as a global marketplace, establishes policies and guidelines to ensure a safe, fair, and transparent environment for buyers and sellers. Staying compliant with these policies is critical for several reasons:

Reputation and Trustworthiness:

Buyer Confidence: Compliance reassures buyers that they are engaging with reputable and trustworthy sellers, encouraging more transactions.

Positive Seller Image: A consistent record of adherence to eBay's policies enhances a seller's reputation and can lead to increased sales and positive feedback.

Seller Performance Standards:

Top-Rated Status: Compliant sellers are more likely to achieve and maintain eBay's top-rated seller status, unlocking benefits like discounts, better exposure, and increased visibility.

Search Rankings: Adherence to policies positively impacts search rankings, boosting visibility in eBay's search results.

Reduced Risk of Account Restrictions or Suspension:

Policy Violation Risks: Non-compliance with eBay's policies can lead to penalties, account restrictions, or suspension, impacting a seller's ability to conduct business on the platform.

Loss of Trust: Violations can erode buyer trust, resulting in negative feedback or loss of sales opportunities.

Buyer Protection and Satisfaction:

Confidence in Transactions: Compliance ensures adherence to standards that protect buyers from fraud, counterfeit items, or misleading listings, fostering a positive buying experience.

Reduced Disputes: Following policies minimizes the likelihood of disputes or conflicts arising from inaccurate listings or misrepresented products.

Legal and Regulatory Compliance:

Legal Obligations: eBay's policies often align with legal requirements, ensuring sellers operate within the bounds of local, national, and international laws.

Risk Mitigation: Compliance reduces the risk of legal action or penalties stemming from violations of consumer protection laws or regulations.

Marketplace Integrity and Fairness:

Level Playing Field: Adherence to policies maintains fairness and integrity within the marketplace, ensuring all sellers compete on a level playing field.

Trust in the Platform: Buyers and sellers trust eBay more when they know policies are consistently enforced, creating a healthier marketplace ecosystem.

CHAPTER SEVEN

Advanced Techniques for Success

Thriving as an eBay seller requires a nuanced approach that goes beyond basic practices. Leveraging advanced techniques and strategies empowers sellers to maximize visibility, optimize sales, and build a robust brand presence within the dynamic marketplace.

1. Fine-Tuning Listing Optimization:

Advanced SEO Practices: Implement targeted keywords, long-tail phrases, and strategic placement to enhance search visibility within eBay's algorithm.
Structured Data Markup: Leverage structured data to optimize listings for search engines, increasing external visibility and attracting more buyers.

2. Dynamic Pricing Strategies:

AI-Powered Pricing Tools: Utilize sophisticated pricing software or algorithms that adapt pricing in real-time based on market demand, competitor pricing, and buyer behavior.
Segmented Pricing: Implement segmented pricing strategies based on buyer demographics, browsing behavior, or purchasing history for targeted pricing.

3. Enhanced Product Presentation:

360-Degree Imaging: Offer immersive product experiences with 360-degree images or videos to provide buyers with a comprehensive view of the item.
Augmented Reality (AR) Integration: Experiment with AR technology to allow buyers to visualize products in their environment before purchase.

4. Customized Marketing Strategies:

Segmented Email Campaigns: Implement targeted email campaigns based on buyer preferences, past purchases, or browsing behavior for personalized engagement.

Social Media Integration: Integrate eBay listings into social media platforms to expand reach and engage potential buyers beyond the eBay ecosystem.

5. Expansion into Cross-Border Trade:

Global Shipping Program: Leverage eBay's Global Shipping Program or other international shipping solutions to tap into global markets and increase sales.

Localization and Cultural Sensitivity: Tailor listings and marketing efforts to resonate with diverse international audiences, considering cultural nuances and preferences.

6. Advanced Data Analytics and Insights:

Predictive Analytics: Utilize predictive analytics to forecast trends, demand, and pricing strategies, optimizing inventory and sales projections.

Buyer Behavior Analysis: Deep dive into buyer behavior data to identify patterns, preferences, and opportunities for targeted marketing and product offerings.

7. Embrace Multi-Channel Selling:

Multi-Platform Integration: Expand beyond eBay by integrating inventory and sales across multiple platforms or marketplaces for broader reach and increased sales opportunities.

Omni-Channel Experience: Ensure consistency in branding, customer service, and product offerings across all channels for a seamless buyer experience.

8. Automation and Workflow Optimization:

Automated Order Processing: Implement automation tools for streamlined order fulfillment, reducing processing times and enhancing efficiency.

AI-Powered Customer Service: Explore AI-driven customer service solutions for faster response times and personalized interactions.

9. Collaboration and Partnerships:

Strategic Partnerships: Collaborate with complementary businesses or influencers for cross-promotions, enhancing visibility and attracting new buyers.

Supplier Negotiations: Strengthen relationships with suppliers for better pricing, exclusivity, or access to unique products.

10. Continuous Learning and Adaptation:

Market Research and Trend Analysis: Stay updated with market trends, emerging technologies, and shifts in buyer behavior for proactive adjustments to strategies.

Experimentation and Innovation: Encourage a culture of experimentation and innovation, testing new tactics and tools to stay ahead in a competitive landscape.

Cross-Promotions and Bundling Strategies, Expanding to International Markets, Exploring eBay's Advanced Features

eBay remains a powerhouse for online commerce, offering an array of opportunities for sellers to expand, innovate, and reach a global audience. Beyond standard practices, advanced strategies like cross-promotions and bundling, international expansion, and leveraging eBay's sophisticated features can propel sellers towards heightened success.

Cross-Promotions and Bundling Strategies

In a competitive marketplace, cross-promotions and product bundling emerge as potent strategies to boost sales and enhance customer value. Cross-promotions involve marketing one product alongside another, while bundling entails offering complementary items as a package deal.

Cross-Promotions:
Cross-promotions on eBay involve showcasing related products to customers while they browse or make a purchase. Utilize eBay's "Related Items" feature to display complementary products, encouraging additional purchases and elevating the shopping experience.

Bundling Strategies:
Create attractive bundle offerings by pairing related items that enhance each other's utility or appeal. Bundling can entice buyers with discounts, convenience, or a perceived added value, encouraging them to purchase more items together.

Expanding to International Markets

eBay's global platform offers sellers an unparalleled opportunity to expand their reach beyond domestic borders. Expanding into international markets involves strategic planning, localization efforts, and understanding diverse customer preferences.

Global Shipping Program:
Leverage eBay's Global Shipping Program to simplify international shipping. This feature streamlines the process, making it easier for sellers

to ship items globally while eBay handles customs and international tracking.

Localization and Cultural Sensitivity:
Tailor listings to resonate with international buyers by considering cultural nuances, language preferences, and local market demands. Localization efforts, including translated listings and localized marketing, can significantly boost visibility and sales in international markets.

Exploring eBay's Advanced Features

eBay offers a suite of advanced features and tools that empower sellers to optimize their listings, improve customer engagement, and maximize sales potential.

Promoted Listings:
Utilize eBay's Promoted Listings feature to boost visibility for select products. This paid tool places items prominently in search results, increasing exposure and potentially driving higher sales.

Structured Data and SEO Enhancement:
Optimize listings using structured data to improve search visibility within eBay and external search engines. Strategic keyword placement, clear titles, and detailed descriptions bolster SEO, ensuring better discoverability.

AI-Powered Insights and Analytics:
Leverage eBay's advanced analytics tools, harnessing predictive insights and buyer behavior data to forecast trends, optimize pricing strategies, and tailor marketing efforts for maximum impact.

CHAPTER EIGHT

Tips for Growth and Sustainability

1. Strategic Listing Optimization:

Craft compelling titles and descriptions with relevant keywords to enhance visibility in search results.

Utilize high-quality images from various angles to showcase products effectively.

Leverage eBay's item specifics and structured data to ensure accurate categorization and details.

2. Competitive Pricing Strategies:

Research market trends and competitor pricing to set competitive yet profitable prices.

Experiment with different pricing models like auctions, fixed-price listings, or Best Offer to gauge buyer interest.

3. Exceptional Customer Service:

Respond promptly to inquiries, address concerns, and resolve issues professionally and efficiently.

Maintain transparency in communication and uphold a high standard of service to foster buyer trust.

4. Optimize Shipping and Returns:

Offer fast and reliable shipping options, utilizing tracking and providing estimated delivery times.

Clearly outline return policies, making the process hassle-free for buyers to build confidence.

5. Utilize Promotional Tools:

Consider eBay's Promoted Listings to increase product visibility and reach a broader audience.
Implement sales promotions, discounts, or bundling offers to incentivize purchases.

6. International Expansion:

Leverage eBay's Global Shipping Program or explore direct international shipping to tap into a wider customer base.
Tailor listings and policies for different markets, considering cultural and regional preferences.

7. Continuous Improvement and Adaptation:

Analyze performance metrics, customer feedback, and sales data to identify areas for improvement.
Adapt strategies, update inventory, and refine practices based on market changes and buyer behavior.

8. Stay Compliant with eBay Policies:

Ensure adherence to eBay's policies, safeguarding against penalties or account limitations.
Uphold high ethical standards in listings, communication, and transactions.

9. Brand Building and Marketing:

Develop a strong brand identity through consistent branding, packaging, and messaging.
Utilize social media or external marketing channels to drive traffic to eBay listings.

10. Build Trust with Positive Feedback:

Encourage buyers to leave feedback after a successful transaction to build a solid reputation.

Address negative feedback professionally and seek resolutions to showcase commitment to customer satisfaction.

By implementing these tips, eBay sellers can enhance their performance, increase sales, and establish a sustainable and thriving presence on the platform.

Building a Long-Term eBay Selling Strategy

Developing a long-term eBay selling strategy involves careful planning, adaptation, and a focus on sustainable growth. Here's a guide to building a robust long-term strategy:

1. Define Your Goals and Objectives:

Establish clear and measurable goals for your eBay business, such as sales targets, market expansion, or brand building.

Outline specific objectives, whether it's increasing product listings, expanding into new categories, or improving customer satisfaction.

2. Conduct Market Research and Analysis:

Research market trends, competitor strategies, and buyer behavior to identify opportunities and niches.

Analyze eBay's data tools to understand what sells well, pricing trends, and emerging product categories.

3. Develop a Brand Identity and Value Proposition:

Craft a unique brand identity that resonates with your target audience through consistent branding, messaging, and quality service.
Define your value proposition—what makes your products or service stand out in the marketplace.

4. Optimize Listings and Product Presentation:

Create compelling listings with clear titles, detailed descriptions, and high-quality images to attract buyers' attention.
Implement structured data, SEO practices, and item specifics to enhance visibility in eBay's search results.

5. Implement Pricing and Sales Strategies:

Develop pricing strategies that balance competitiveness with profitability, considering market trends and buyer expectations.
Experiment with different sales tactics such as promotions, discounts, or bundling to stimulate sales and attract custo

6. Focus on Exceptional Customer Service:

Prioritize customer satisfaction by providing prompt and courteous responses to inquiries and addressing issues efficiently.
Offer transparent and hassle-free return policies to build trust and confidence among buyers.

7. Leverage eBay's Tools and Features:

Utilize eBay's analytics, promoted listings, and seller hub to gain insights, optimize performance, and increase visibility.
Explore advanced features like AI-powered insights or multi-channel selling options for broader reach and efficiency.

8. Adaptability and Continuous Improvement:

Stay agile and adaptable to changing market conditions, buyer preferences, and eBay policy updates.
Regularly evaluate performance metrics, feedback, and sales data to identify areas for improvement and innovation.

9. Expand and Diversify Smartly:

Expand your product range or enter new markets cautiously, considering profitability, demand, and potential risks.
Diversify your inventory strategically, catering to different customer needs while aligning with your brand identity.

10. Long-Term Sustainability and Growth:

Aim for sustainable growth by balancing short-term gains with long-term stability and scalability.
Foster relationships with loyal customers, suppliers, and partners to create a robust and enduring business ecosystem.

By crafting a well-defined long-term eBay selling strategy that encompasses these elements, sellers can navigate the marketplace effectively, adapt to evolving trends, and build a resilient and prosperous eBay business over time.

Adapting to Market Changes, Diversifying Your Product Offerings

These steps are to be followed if you as a seller wishes to adapt to market changes and Diversify your product offerings

1. Monitor Market Trends and Buyer Behavior:

Stay informed about shifts in consumer preferences, emerging trends, and market dynamics using eBay's analytics tools and external market research.
Track changes in demand, seasonality, or trending product categories to anticipate shifts in buyer behavior.

2. Flexibility and Agility in Product Offerings:

Be adaptable and agile in adjusting product offerings to align with changing market demands or seasonal trends.
Rotate inventory, introduce new products, or modify existing listings based on market shifts to maintain relevance.

3. Expand into Complementary Product Lines:

Identify related or complementary product categories that align with your brand and existing offerings.
Diversify by adding products that cater to the same target audience or solve related needs.

4. Test New Products or Variations:

Experiment with new product lines, variations, or limited-time offerings to gauge buyer interest and test market viability.
Use eBay's testing tools or run pilot programs to assess the performance and potential of new additions.

5. Strategic Bundling and Cross-Selling:

Create bundled packages by combining related products or offering discounts for multiple purchases to encourage upselling.
Cross-sell by showcasing related items within listings or utilizing eBay's 'Frequently Bought Together' feature.

6. Leverage Seasonal and Trend-based Opportunities:

Capitalize on seasonal events, holidays, or trending themes by adapting product offerings and marketing campaigns accordingly.
Align promotions, discounts, or themed listings with seasonal trends to attract seasonal shoppers.

7. Solicit Customer Feedback and Insights:

Engage with buyers for feedback on existing products, potential offerings, or features they'd like to see.
Use surveys, polls, or follow-up communication to gather insights and adapt offerings based on customer preferences.

8. Research and Explore Niche Markets:

Identify untapped or niche markets within your industry that present opportunities for growth.
Explore specialized products or niche segments to cater to specific buyer interests or unmet needs.

9. Collaborate or Source from New Suppliers:

Establish partnerships or source products from new suppliers to access a wider range of offerings.
Seek suppliers that offer unique or exclusive products to differentiate your inventory.

10. Continuous Evaluation and Optimization:

Regularly review the performance of new product additions or variations using eBay's analytics.
Optimize listings, pricing, and marketing strategies based on data insights and performance metrics.

GLOSSARY

A glossary is a reference section that provides explanations, definitions, or descriptions of specialized or unfamiliar terms used within a particular context. Here is a glossary related to the eBay marketplace:

Buy It Now (BIN): An option allowing buyers to purchase an item immediately at a fixed price without participating in an auction.

Reserve Price: The minimum price set by a seller in an auction, below which they are not obliged to sell the item.

Starting Bid: The initial price set by a seller when listing an item for auction.

Bid Increment: The minimum amount by which a bid must increase each time a new bid is placed on an auction item.

Auction Duration: The specified period during which an auction remains open for bidding before closing.

Highest Bidder: The buyer who has placed the highest bid on an auction item before it closes.

Buyer Protection: eBay's program that safeguards buyers from fraudulent sellers or misrepresented items.

Seller Protection: eBay's program that offers protection to sellers against issues such as unpaid items or fraudulent buyer claims.

Feedback Score: A numerical score reflecting a user's reputation on eBay, based on feedback received from transactions.

Item Condition Definitions: Terms such as "New," "Used," "Refurbished," etc., indicating the condition of an item listed on eBay.

Best Offer: An option allowing buyers to negotiate a lower price with the seller for a fixed-price item.

Promoted Listings: A feature allowing sellers to pay for increased visibility of their items in search results.

Handling Time: The duration within which a seller commits to shipping an item after receiving payment.

Return Policy: A seller's policy detailing the conditions under which buyers can return items for a refund.

Shipping Options: Different methods available for shipping items, such as standard, expedited, or express shipping.

eBay Store: A subscription-based service offering sellers a dedicated online storefront to showcase and sell their products.

Watch List: A feature enabling users to track items they are interested in, without placing a bid or committing to buy.

PowerSeller: A designation for sellers who consistently meet high sales volume and customer service standards on eBay.

Top-Rated Seller: A status awarded to sellers who consistently provide excellent service and meet specific performance criteria.

Global Shipping Program (GSP): eBay's program facilitating international shipping for sellers, managing customs and international tracking.

FAQS

These FAQs cover common queries encountered by eBay users, providing essential information about buying, selling, fees, policies, and more within the eBay marketplace.

1. What is eBay?

eBay is an online marketplace that connects buyers and sellers worldwide. It facilitates the sale of a wide range of products through auction-style bidding or fixed-price listings.

2. How do I create an eBay account?

To create an eBay account, visit the eBay website and click on "Register" or "Sign Up." Fill in your personal information, choose a username, and create a password. Follow the prompts to verify your email address and complete the registration process.

3. How do I buy items on eBay?

Find the item you want to purchase by searching or browsing eBay's listings. Click on the item, review the details, and if satisfied, click "Buy It Now" (for fixed-price items) or place a bid (for auctions). Follow the prompts to complete the purchase.

4. How do I sell items on eBay?

To sell on eBay, create a listing by providing details about your item, including title, description, price, and photos. Set your selling format (auction or fixed price) and shipping options. Once listed, manage inquiries, and ship the item upon sale.

5. What fees does eBay charge sellers?

eBay charges sellers various fees, including an insertion fee for listing items and a final value fee based on the item's sale price. Additional fees may apply for optional features, such as promoted listings or upgrades.

6. How does bidding work on eBay?

Bidding on eBay involves placing your maximum bid amount on an auction item. Other buyers can then place higher bids, and eBay's system automatically increases your bid incrementally until your maximum is reached or the auction ends.

7. What is the eBay Money Back Guarantee?

The eBay Money Back Guarantee ensures that buyers receive the item they ordered or get their money back. It covers most purchases made on eBay and provides protection against items not received or significantly not as described.

8. Can I cancel a bid on eBay?

In most cases, bids on eBay are binding contracts, and retracting a bid is discouraged. However, under specific circumstances, such as making a typo in the bid amount, eBay may allow bid retraction within certain limits.

9. How do I leave feedback on eBay?

After a transaction, both buyers and sellers can leave feedback for each other. Go to the "Feedback" section on your eBay account, select the transaction, and choose a rating and comment based on your experience.

10. How do I contact eBay customer service?

eBay offers various customer service options, including live chat, email support, and a customer service hotline. You can find the contact information by visiting the eBay Help & Contact section on their website.

11. Is it safe to buy items on eBay?

eBay has various buyer protection programs in place, such as the Money Back Guarantee, which offer safeguards against fraudulent sellers or misrepresented items. Always check seller ratings and reviews before making a purchase.

12. Can I negotiate prices on eBay?

eBay offers a "Best Offer" feature on some listings, allowing buyers to propose a price lower than the listed amount. Sellers can accept, decline, or counter the offer.

13. What happens if I don't pay for an item I won in an auction?

Not paying for a won auction item is considered a violation of eBay policy and can result in penalties, such as a strike on your account. Repeated violations may lead to account suspension.

14. Are there restrictions on what I can sell on eBay?

eBay has guidelines and restrictions on items that can be sold, including prohibited items like weapons, illegal products, or certain regulated goods. Review eBay's prohibited and restricted items policy before listing.

15. How do I track my eBay order?
Once a seller ships your item, they usually provide a tracking number. You can track the package's status by entering the tracking number into the shipping carrier's website or through eBay's order details.

16. Can I sell internationally on eBay?

Yes, eBay allows sellers to offer their items to international buyers. Sellers can opt into the Global Shipping Program or choose to ship items directly to international destinations.

17. What is an eBay Store, and do I need one to sell?

An eBay Store is a subscription-based service that provides sellers with a dedicated storefront to showcase and sell their products. It offers additional tools and benefits but is not necessary for selling on eBay.

18. How long do I have to wait for an auction to end?

The duration of an auction on eBay can vary. Sellers can set the auction duration, typically ranging from 1 to 10 days. The specific auction end time is mentioned in the listing.

19. Can I change or cancel a listing after it's posted?

Sellers can edit some aspects of a listing, such as item description or price, while it's active. However, canceling a listing prematurely may incur fees and impact seller performance.

20. How do I report suspicious or fraudulent activity on eBay?

If you encounter suspicious activity or believe you've come across a fraudulent listing or seller, you can report it to eBay's customer service through the "Report item" or "Contact Us" options on the website.